I0475132

LEMONADE FOR SALE

A Guide to Nurturing the Spirit of Entrepreneurship

Daniel H. Sohn

Copyright

Title: Lemonade for Sale

Subtitle: A Guide to Nurturing the Spirit of Entrepreneurship

Author & Publisher: Daniel H. Sohn

Foreword by: Jeremy Ring

Copyright Year: © 2024 Daniel H. Sohn

ISBN: 978-1-300-73771-1

All rights reserved. No part of this book may be reproduced in any form or by any electronic or mechanical means, including photocopying, recording, or information storage and retrieval systems, without the prior written permission of the publisher, except for the use of brief quotations in a book review or scholarly journal.

Distributor:

Lulu Press, Inc.

https://www.lulu.com/

Dedication

This book is dedicated to every young dreamer whose first big idea started with a lemonade stand.

This book is for you.

Foreword

"Some of us dared to dream big, while others just did what was necessary to keep the lights on. But it was those willing to embrace the chaos who ultimately reshaped the world." — We Were Yahoo!

Entrepreneurship is about creating something from nothing, daring to innovate, and having the courage to adapt when faced with the unexpected. As one of Yahoo's early team members, I witnessed firsthand the magic of bold ideas and the power of turning simple concepts into transformative ventures.

Lemonade for Sale: A Guide to Nurturing the Spirit of Entrepreneurship captures that same energy and distills it into a framework accessible to everyone. Using the lemonade stand, a symbol of grassroots entrepreneurship. This book speaks to young dreamers, parents cultivating entrepreneurial values, and first-time business owners. It takes the reader on a journey through the essential elements of launching and growing a business, from resilience to teamwork, creativity to legacy-building.

In these pages, you'll find not just advice but inspiration. Entrepreneurship isn't linear; it's messy, challenging, and deeply rewarding. Lemonade for Sale invites you to embrace those challenges, turn setbacks into opportunities, and build something that reflects your unique vision. Whether your goal is a lemonade stand or the next tech giant, the lessons here will empower you to start small but think big.

This book reminds us all that the entrepreneurial spirit isn't confined to boardrooms or billion-dollar valuations—it begins at the simplest, most human level: with an idea and the will to make it real. So grab this guide, step forward with confidence, and remember: every great business starts with a single drop of lemonade.

— JEREMY RING,

Former Senator, Yahoo Executive

& Author Of We Were Yahoo!

About the Author

Daniel H. Sohn is an award-winning business leader and advocate with a distinguished career in chamber of commerce management, economic development, and workforce development advocacy. Over the years, he has served as the CEO of multiple chambers of commerce and business associations, where he successfully advanced initiatives to strengthen local economies, support small businesses and foster vibrant communities.

With a proven track record in non-profit leadership and destination marketing, Daniel has earned accolades for his innovative approach to building partnerships and driving meaningful change. His commitment to empowering businesses and enhancing economic opportunities has made him a sought-after advisor and consultant in the industry.

Through *Lemonade for Sale: A Guide to Nurturing the Spirit of Entrepreneurship*, Daniel shares his insights to empower aspiring entrepreneurs with the tools, resilience, and vision to succeed.

For more about Daniel's work, achievements, and ongoing projects, visit www.danielsohn.com.

Table of Contents

Dedication iii

Foreword iv

About the Author vi

Table of Contents vii

Introduction ix

Chapter 1 1

The Spark of Inspiration 1

Chapter 2 8

Gathering Ingredients 8

Chapter 3 17

Squeezing the Lemons 17

Chapter 4 32

Stirring the Sweetness 32

Chapter 5 43

Setting Up Shop 43

Chapter 6 55

The First Pour 55

Chapter 7   65

Making Lemonade from Lemons   65

Chapter 8   78

Leaving a Legacy   78

Chapter 9   87

Conclusion   87

Introduction

What is it about a humble glass of lemonade that feels so familiar and inviting? It's simple, refreshing, and a little nostalgic reminding us of summer days, childhood ambitions, and the entrepreneurial dreams that start small but hold big possibilities.

Do you remember the thrill of selling something as a kid? Perhaps it was lemonade on a sunny day, a simple stand, and a smiling child selling freshly squeezed lemonade to passersby. The lemonade stand is an iconic symbol of entrepreneurship where many of us first encounter the thrill of running a business. It's more than just a childhood memory; it's a symbol of the entrepreneurial journey. Each glass of lemonade represents creativity, effort, and the courage to turn a simple idea into something tangible.

Entrepreneurship, much like making lemonade, starts with humble ingredients—lemons, sugar, water, and a dash of determination. These ingredients mirror the essentials of building a business: a vision (lemons), hard work (squeezing and mixing), strategy (balancing flavors), and resilience (weathering the occasional storm). No matter where you are in life, the principles of a lemonade stand—creativity, adaptability, and customer focus—are universally relevant.

The truth is that starting a business is not always easy. Sometimes, the lemons life hands us are sourer than expected. What if no one stops to buy? What if it rains? What if your lemons run out? These "what-ifs" often keep potential entrepreneurs from taking the leap. And that's exactly why this book exists.

One of the greatest privileges I have as a Chamber of Commerce Executive is witnessing the growth of entrepreneurs over time. Each business owner comes to the chamber at a different stage of their journey—some are just launching their companies, others are hiring their first employees, expanding to new locations, or proudly unveiling their first logo or business card. It's such a joy to share in their milestones, whether it's a ribbon-cutting, anniversary, or reopening. Entrepreneurs truly make the world a better place, and I feel incredibly fortunate to be part of their success!

Lemonade for Sale: A Guide to Nurturing the Spirit of Entrepreneurship isn't just a book; it's your mentor, cheerleader, toolkit, and action planner wrapped into one. Whether you're a young entrepreneur dreaming big, a parent nurturing your child's entrepreneurial spark, or someone starting their first business, this guide is for you.

At age 3, *Ryan Hickman* noticed that he was bothered by the sight of trashy bottles scattered on the ground, prompting him to gather recyclables from his family and neighbors, which eventually evolved into his own business. According to *Arturo Henriquez* a seasoned business acquirer, the lessons learned from childhood ventures like lemonade stands play a pivotal role in fostering creativity, resilience, and adaptability later in life.

This book will walk you through every stage of building a business, using the lemonade stand as a reference to simplify even the most complex concepts. From finding inspiration to facing challenges and leaving a legacy, you'll learn the fundamentals of entrepreneurship in an engaging, digestible, and practical way.

For every success story, there are tales of struggle, fear, and doubt. According to research published in the *Harvard Business Review*, a significant portion of aspiring entrepreneurs identify "fear of failure" as the primary obstacle preventing them from pursuing their entrepreneurial ambitions. This finding suggests that this fear is a major psychological barrier for many individuals considering starting a business.

Let's rewind to when I was 8 years old. With a folding table, a hand-drawn sign, and a jug of lemonade, I set up my first business on the corner of my block. I was confident until the first hour passed without a single customer. My confidence turned into frustration. "Why isn't anyone stopping?" I thought. But instead of giving up, I adjusted my strategy. I moved my stand closer to the playground, where parents and kids passed by. And guess what? The second glass I poured was for a mom who bought five cups for her kids and their friends. That was my first taste of entrepreneurship and the power of persistence.

This book does not focus on how to get rich quickly or promise overnight success. Instead, it equips you with tools and mindsets that work for anyone willing to start. We'll explore how to turn ideas into action, even if you feel stuck or uncertain. Build the skills that entrepreneurs need: problem-solving, creativity, and communication. Overcome challenges and setbacks with resilience and resourcefulness and use modern tools like social media, e-commerce platforms, and digital marketing to grow your business.

If you're a parent, you'll learn how to empower your children with life lessons from entrepreneurship, teaching them accountability, teamwork, and the value of money.

For first-time entrepreneurs, I'll tackle your fears head-on. Starting something new is daunting, but with the right guidance, it's also exhilarating.

This book simplifies what can feel overwhelming. Every business concept I discuss will tie back to the idea of running a lemonade stand—approachable, fun, and memorable. But don't mistake simplicity for lack of depth. Alongside real-life stories and practical advice, this book incorporates research-backed strategies, reflective exercises, and modern examples to help you succeed in today's dynamic business world.

So, are you ready to grab your lemons and make something extraordinary? Let's roll up our sleeves and turn dreams into action. As we explore the world of lemonade, you'll discover that entrepreneurship is great—it helps create value, solve problems, and leave a lasting impact.

Are you ready? Let's get started.

Chapter 1

The Spark of Inspiration

In the vast and often unpredictable business landscape, one fundamental truth stands out consistently: every great endeavor begins with a spark of inspiration. This is the pivotal moment when a seemingly ordinary concept evolves into a vivid vision, a beacon that illuminates the path forward. It is this vision that ignites decisive action, propelling individuals and teams toward their goals. The spark of inspiration acts as a powerful, yet invisible force, driving some of the most transformative and groundbreaking ventures in history. It highlights the potential within each idea, reminding us that even the simplest thought can lead to remarkable change when fueled by creativity and passion.

From Steve Jobs envisioning Apple in a garage to Oprah Winfrey building a media empire rooted in connection, the story is often the same. Success is born not from elaborate plans but from a single spark of an idea that excites, challenges, and motivates. But how do you find that spark, and once found, how do you nurture it into something meaningful?

This chapter will unpack the essence of inspiration in entrepreneurship: its origins, how it drives creativity, and practical steps to help you discover yours. Whether you're a young entrepreneur, a parent guiding a child, or someone taking their first leap into business, inspiration is your starting point.

What Is the Spark of Inspiration?

The spark of inspiration is more than just a fleeting thought. It's a moment of clarity when an idea aligns with your passions, challenges your abilities, and propels you to act. Creativity and passion fuel inspiration, acting as catalysts for entrepreneurial breakthroughs.

Inspiration often comes from unexpected places. It's the creative energy that emerges when observing a problem, brainstorming solutions, or simply letting your mind wander. For instance, Howard Schultz was inspired to turn Starbucks into a coffeehouse experience after a trip to Italy. His spark? Observing the community-building role of Italian espresso bars.

Inspiration is not solely about big ideas. Sometimes, it's the simple realization that you can do something better, faster, or more meaningfully.

Where Does Inspiration Come From?

1. **Challenges and Frustrations**

   Problems are the seeds of great ideas. Think about the last time something frustrated you. Could you solve that issue for others? Sara Blakely founded Spanx because she couldn't find comfortable undergarments that suited her needs. Similarly, many local businesses begin as solutions to community-specific problems.

Action Step: Write down three things that frustrate you in your daily life. For each, brainstorm one potential solution.

2. **Passions and Hobbies**

Passion transforms work into joy. Hobbies are fertile ground for entrepreneurial inspiration because they reflect what you genuinely love. Walt Disney's passion for storytelling and art led to the creation of a global empire that continues to inspire generations.

Kevin Plank started Under Armour because he was tired of sweat-soaked cotton shirts during football practice. His passion for sports led him to develop moisture-wicking athletic wear that became a game-changer.

3. **Community Needs**

Sometimes, inspiration comes from observing unmet needs in your environment. Mikaila Ulmer's lemonade stand began with a mission: saving bees. She saw the decline in bee populations as a problem worth solving and used her platform to educate while running a profitable business.

4. **Serendipity and Curiosity**

Keep your eyes open. Inspiration often strikes in moments of curiosity or through unexpected encounters. According to Utley, brainstorming and creative exercises encourage this type of spontaneous insight.

Tip: Engage in diverse experiences—travel, read widely, and interact with people outside your usual circle.

The Role of Parents in Cultivating Inspiration

Parents are pivotal in nurturing the entrepreneurial spirit in children. Early exposure to creativity, problem-solving, and resilience can lay a foundation for success.

1. **Encouraging Curiosity**

   Ask open-ended questions. When your child faces a challenge, instead of offering a solution, ask, *"What do you think we should do?"* This fosters critical thinking.

2. **Providing Resources**

   A lemonade stand might seem simple, but it teaches budgeting, marketing, and customer service. Equip your child with tools that allow them to experiment with entrepreneurship.

3. **Highlighting Role Models**

   Share stories of young entrepreneurs to inspire your child. For example, Ryan Hickman began a recycling business at age seven, demonstrating that age is no barrier to success.

4. **Celebrating Effort Over Outcome**

   Praise persistence and effort, not just achievements. This helps children develop a growth mindset, which is essential for tackling challenges.

Exercises to Find Your Spark

For young entrepreneurs and beginners alike, these activities can help identify passions and opportunities:

1. **Problem Journal:**

   Over the next week, jot down every inconvenience or frustration you encounter. At the end of the week, choose one and brainstorm ways to address it.

2. **Hobby Exploration:**

   List your favorite hobbies and ask, *"How could I turn this into a product or service?"*

3. **Community Observation:**

   Spend time in your neighborhood or community. Look for gaps—services or products that are missing.

4. **Passion Map:**

   Create a visual map connecting your interests, skills, and values. Look for intersections that spark excitement.

Steps to Nurture Inspiration

Inspiration is only the beginning. To turn an idea into reality, you need focus and commitment.

1. **Validate Your Idea**

   Share your idea with friends or mentors. Gather feedback and refine your concept.

2. **Start Small**

   Test your idea on a small scale. If your spark is a product, create a prototype. If it's a service, offer it to a few people for feedback.

3. **Stay Curious**

   Inspiration isn't a one-time event. Continually expose yourself to new ideas and experiences to fuel your creativity.

4. **Embrace Failure**

   Every successful entrepreneur has stories of failed ideas. Treat setbacks as opportunities to learn and improve.

Case Study: Airbnb's Spark

Brian Chesky and Joe Gebbia couldn't afford rent in San Francisco. Their simple solution? Renting out air mattresses in their apartment. This small, seemingly quirky idea grew into Airbnb, now valued at over $100 billion. Their story underscores the power of testing small ideas and iterating based on feedback.

Inspiration does not occur by chance; rather, it is cultivated through a mindset characterized by openness, curiosity, and a willingness to engage with a variety of experiences. When individuals actively seek out new perspectives and challenge their existing beliefs, they create a rich environment conducive to inspiration. Engaging in activities such as journaling allows for personal reflection and the exploration of thoughts and feelings, providing clarity and insights that can spark new ideas. Brainstorming sessions enable the free flow of creativity, encouraging individuals to think outside the box and consider unconventional solutions. Reflective thinking, which involves analyzing past experiences and understanding their impact, helps to connect dots that may not have been apparent at first. Together, these practices nurture a fertile ground where inspiration can take root and thrive, transforming fleeting thoughts into powerful creations. *Nexford University* (2024) emphasizes that an entrepreneurial mindset, characterized by resilience and risk-taking, amplifies the likelihood of acting on inspiration.

The spark of inspiration is the beginning of every entrepreneurial journey. But inspiration alone isn't enough; it must be nurtured and acted upon. In the next chapter, *"Gathering Ingredients,"* we'll explore how to transform your idea into a plan, identifying the resources, skills, and strategies you need to succeed.

As you move forward, remember: your spark has the potential to illuminate not just your path but also inspire others to dream, create, and achieve. Are you ready to take the next step? Let's turn your inspiration into action!

Chapter 2

Gathering Ingredients

In the world of business, success often hinges upon the ability to gather the right ingredients. Just as a chef selects the freshest produce for a delectable dish, a savvy entrepreneur meticulously gathers the essential elements for a thriving venture. The parallels are undeniable without the right components: vision, skills, resources, mindset, and passion, the recipe for success can fall flat.

This chapter delves deep into what it means to "gather ingredients" in entrepreneurship. By the end of this chapter, you will understand the importance of these elements and have actionable strategies to begin assembling your own toolkit for success.

The Core Ingredients for Business Success

1. **Vision**

   Every successful entrepreneur begins with a clear vision. It's your North Star—the guiding light that keeps you aligned with your goals and objectives. Without a crystal-clear understanding of your destination, you risk drifting aimlessly.

   Why It Matters:

   Vision fuels your drive and ensures that every decision aligns with your ultimate purpose. It helps you prioritize, focus, and communicate your goals effectively.

Example: Elon Musk's vision for SpaceX was to make life multi-planetary. This audacious goal set the company apart, also attracted the best talent and investors.

Action Point: Write down your vision in one sentence. For example: *"I want to create a sustainable clothing brand that empowers local artisans and reduces environmental impact."* Revisit this vision regularly to ensure alignment.

2. **Skills**

Skills are the practical tools that allow you to bring your vision to life. Whether you're a tech-savvy coder or a natural salesperson, honing your skills is essential.

How to Identify Key Skills:

- o **Personal Assessment:** Reflect on what you're naturally good at.

- o **Seek Feedback:** Ask colleagues, friends, or mentors about your strengths.

- o **Continuous Learning:** Take courses, attend workshops, or read industry-specific books.

For Parents: Encourage your children to explore different activities to discover their strengths. Offer opportunities for them to develop these skills through hobbies, sports, or creative projects.

3. **Resources:**

Resources encompass everything from finances and tools to networks and knowledge. While financial capital is crucial, other resources like mentorship and access to technology can be equally transformative.

Tips for Gathering Resources:

- o Bootstrap where possible to minimize risk.

- o Reach out to friends, family, or alumni groups for support.

- o Explore Grants and Competitions: Many organizations offer funding or resources for startups.

Example: Dropbox founder Drew Houston used his MIT alumni network to gain early traction and mentorship.

Checklist:

- o Have you identified potential funding sources?

- o Do you have access to the tools and technology needed for your business?

- o Are there mentors or advisors who can guide you?

4. **Mindset**

A resilient and growth-oriented mindset is non-negotiable in entrepreneurship. Challenges will arise, and your ability to adapt and persevere will determine your success.

Developing a Resilient Mindset:

- o **Embrace Failure:** Treat setbacks as opportunities to learn and grow.

- o **Practice Positivity:** Focus on solutions rather than dwelling on problems.

- o **Stay Curious:** Continuously seek out new ideas and perspectives.

As Thomas Edison said, *"I have not failed. I've just found 10,000 ways that won't work."*

Guidance for Parents to Teach Children the Value of Planning

Teaching children the value of planning lays a solid foundation for future entrepreneurial thinking. Planning helps children understand goal-setting, resource allocation, and the importance of preparation. Here are practical ways parents can foster this critical skill:

1. Model Planning in Everyday Life

Children learn by observing adults. Share your planning processes, whether organizing a family trip, creating a grocery budget, or tackling home projects. Demonstrate how planning saves time, reduces stress, and ensures success.

Example Activity: When planning a family outing, involve your child. Discuss how to estimate travel time, budget for expenses, and decide on activities. Ask questions like, *"What could go wrong, and how can we prepare?"*

2. Use Fun, Hands-On Projects

Engage children in simple, fun activities that require planning. A lemonade stand is an excellent starting point. Help your child:

- Decide on a location.

- Budget for supplies.

- Price their product to ensure profitability.

Tip for Younger Children: Use visual aids like charts or drawings to help them grasp the concept of planning.

3. Introduce Tools for Planning

Start with age-appropriate tools.

- **For younger children:** Use calendars, checklists, or sticky notes.

- **For older children:** Introduce digital tools like apps or project management software (e.g., Trello).

Encourage them to plan simple tasks like homework schedules, chore rotations, or holiday gift ideas.

4. Reward the Process, Not Just the Outcome

Celebrate their efforts in planning, even if the results don't pan out as expected. This teaches them to focus on the process and highlights the importance of preparation over immediate success.

Dr. Carol Dweck's research on *growth mindset* emphasizes rewarding effort to build resilience and perseverance in children.

5. Make Mistakes a Learning Opportunity

Planning doesn't always guarantee success. When plans go awry, guide your child in reflecting on what could have been done differently. This builds problem-solving skills and helps them adapt to unexpected situations.

Example for Discussion: *"What didn't work as planned today, and how can we fix it tomorrow?"*

Explore How to Identify Personal Strengths and Market Opportunities

A key to entrepreneurial success is aligning personal strengths with market opportunities. Here's how to identify both:

1. Discover Personal Strengths

Encourage self-awareness by helping children and beginners reflect on their skills and interests.

Practical Steps:

- **Strength Journals:** Ask them to write down tasks they excel at or enjoy.

- **Feedback Loop:** Encourage them to seek input from teachers, friends, or family about their strengths.

- **Personality and Strength Tests:** Use tools like CliftonStrengths or MBTI for older individuals to gain deeper insights.

If a child is great at storytelling, they could explore opportunities like creating a YouTube channel, starting a blog, or even crafting an interactive lemonade stand pitch.

2. Analyze Market Needs

Opportunities often lie where personal strengths intersect with market gaps. Teach children and entrepreneurs to observe their environment critically.

Tips for Identifying Market Needs:

- **Conduct Surveys:** Ask friends and neighbors about unmet needs.

- **Observe Trends:** Study local or global trends to identify emerging demands. For instance, the rise in sustainable products creates opportunities for eco-friendly ventures.

- **Solve Problems:** Encourage thinking about what frustrates them or others. Each frustration is a potential opportunity.

Example: Warby Parker, an eyewear brand, identified a significant gap in the market: affordable yet stylish prescription glasses. Before their entry, many consumers found themselves forced to choose between expensive designer frames and lower-quality, unattractive options.

By observing consumer pain points—particularly the frustration of overpaying for essential eyewear—the founders designed a direct-to-consumer model. This approach allowed them to offer stylish, high-quality frames at a fraction of the cost. Warby Parker also addressed convenience by introducing a home try-on service, which resolved a common frustration with traditional shopping.

3. Leverage Data and Research

Use simple tools like Google Trends or community surveys to gather insights into market behavior. Teach children and beginners to analyze basic data to validate their ideas.

A child notices classmates struggling with organizing homework. They could create a fun, colorful planner to address this gap, starting with surveys to refine the idea.

4. Encourage Experimentation

It's okay to try multiple ideas before settling on one. Encourage children to experiment with different activities or projects to discover where their strengths meet market demands.

Pro Tip: Remind them that successful entrepreneurs often iterate. Jeff Bezos started with books on Amazon before expanding into other markets.

These strategies help build foundational skills in planning, self-awareness, and opportunity identification, ensuring readiness for the entrepreneurial journey.

Reflection and Exercises

1. **Vision Workshop:** Write down your business vision. Ask yourself, *"Why does this matter, and what impact do I want to create?"*

2. **Skills Inventory:** List five skills you excel at and five you'd like to improve. Research ways to develop the latter.

3. **Resource Map:** Create a diagram of your current resources (money, networks, tools). Identify gaps and brainstorm ways to fill them.

Gathering the ingredients for entrepreneurship is a deliberate process. It's about defining your vision, sharpening your skills, leveraging resources, and cultivating the right mindset. Just like a carefully crafted recipe, each component plays a vital role in creating a thriving business.

In the next chapter, *"Squeezing the Lemons,"* we'll explore how to turn challenges into opportunities, learning how to navigate adversity with resilience and innovation. Are you ready to take the next step? Let's dive in!

Chapter 3

Squeezing the Lemons

In business, success often depends on one's ability to adapt and identify opportunities where others see obstacles. Just as squeezing a lemon extracts every ounce of juice, entrepreneurs must approach challenges with creativity, determination, and resourcefulness. Challenges are inevitable, but how you respond to them defines your journey.

This chapter will explore how to transform setbacks into stepping stones. We'll also provide a framework for problem-solving and practical advice for handling uncertainty, ensuring you're equipped to face the inevitable twists and turns of entrepreneurship.

Adapting to Challenges and Turning Setbacks into Opportunities

Entrepreneurship is often a journey marked by obstacles, uncertainties, and unexpected setbacks. Yet, history has shown that challenges can become catalysts for growth and innovation when approached with the right mindset and strategies. Here's how entrepreneurs can adapt to challenges and transform setbacks into opportunities:

1. Shift Perspective

Viewing setbacks as opportunities to innovate or improve is essential. This perspective enables entrepreneurs to identify hidden potential within problems.

As earlier stated, when Airbnb's founders struggled to afford rent, they turned their personal predicament into a solution that disrupted the global hospitality industry. Their "challenge" became the foundation for a multibillion-dollar company.

When faced with a setback, ask yourself:

- *What can I learn from this?*

- *How can this challenge reshape my approach?*

2. Innovate Through Constraints

Limitations often force creativity. Working within constraints can lead to unique solutions that distinguish a business from its competitors. During the 2008 financial crisis, Netflix shifted its focus from DVD rentals to streaming services. The company embraced the technological shift and is now a leading global entertainment platform.

Strategy:

- **Analyze Constraints:** Identify the barriers you're facing.

- **Brainstorm Alternatives:** Think of unconventional ways to overcome those barriers.

3. Embrace the Pivot

Sometimes, setbacks highlight the need for a pivot—a shift in strategy, product, or market focus. Pivoting can rejuvenate a struggling business and open new avenues for success.

Slack, now one of the leading workplace communication tools, began as a failed gaming company. When the original product didn't gain traction, the team pivoted to the internal messaging tool they'd built to manage their own projects.

Action Step:

- Evaluate what's not working.
- Identify core strengths or assets that can be repurposed.
- Test your pivot idea on a small scale before full implementation.

4. Resilience as a Skill

Resilience is the backbone of entrepreneurial success. It involves maintaining focus and optimism in the face of adversity, continuously working toward solutions rather than dwelling on problems.

Insights from Research:

- Studies by *INSEAD* (2024) emphasize resilience as a critical trait in successful entrepreneurs, enabling them to navigate market fluctuations and unexpected setbacks.

- Psychological research highlights that resilient individuals are more likely to maintain motivation and persistence during challenging times.

5. Learn from Feedback and Failure

Feedback, even negative, can guide improvements, while failure often reveals valuable lessons that refine future strategies.

"Success is stumbling from failure to failure with no loss of enthusiasm." — Winston Churchill

James Dyson created 5,126 prototypes before launching his revolutionary vacuum cleaner. Each failed attempt taught him something new, leading to eventual success.

6. Build a Support System

Navigating challenges alone can feel overwhelming. Mentors, peers, and professional networks provide guidance, encouragement, and fresh perspectives.

Action Step:

- Join industry-specific groups or forums.

- Regularly consult with mentors to gain insights on overcoming obstacles.

7. Use Tools and Frameworks

Adopting structured approaches to problem-solving can help in addressing setbacks systematically.

Adapting to challenges is an inevitable part of entrepreneurship. By shifting perspectives, embracing innovation, and staying resilient, setbacks can become stepping stones to success. Each challenge, much like a sour lemon, holds the potential to be transformed into something refreshing and rewarding—like a glass of lemonade.

Framework for Problem-Solving and Resilience

In entrepreneurship, setbacks and challenges are inevitable. Success often depends not on avoiding problems but on addressing them effectively and bouncing back stronger. Below is a structured framework to guide entrepreneurs through problem-solving while building resilience, enabling them to navigate uncertainty with confidence.

Step 1: Define the Problem Clearly

Before solving a problem, it's essential to understand it thoroughly. Misidentifying the issue can lead to wasted resources and frustration.

Key Actions:

- Break the problem into smaller components.

- Ask, *"What is the real issue here?"*

- Use tools like the *"5 Whys" Technique* to uncover root causes. (Example: If sales are declining, keep asking "Why?" until you identify whether it's due to pricing, product relevance, or market competition.)

Elon Musk famously tackled inefficiencies in the aerospace industry by redefining the problem: instead of expensive launches, he focused on reusable rockets. This clarity drove SpaceX's innovative approach.

21

Step 2: Brainstorm and Generate Solutions

Once the problem is clear, shift into solution mode. Creativity and collaboration are vital here.

Key Actions:

- Encourage brainstorming sessions with no judgment.

- Gather input from diverse perspectives, including team members, mentors, and customers.

- Use the SCAMPER Method: It is a problem-solving technique used to generate creative ideas and solutions by encouraging individuals or teams to think about their challenges from different perspectives. SCAMPER stands for Substitute, Combine, Adapt, Modify, Put to another use, Eliminate, and Reverse, each representing a unique approach to ideation.

  o **Substitute:** Replace components, materials, or processes with alternatives. *Example:* Replace plastic with biodegradable materials to create eco-friendly packaging.

  o **Combine:** Merge elements to create something new or improve functionality. *Example*: Smartphones combine a camera, GPS, and computer into one device.

  o **Adapt:** Modify or repurpose an idea to meet new needs or challenges. *Example*: Velcro was inspired by burrs sticking to clothing.

22

- o **Modify:** Alter scale, design, or features for improvement. *Example*: Redesign packaging for sustainability and aesthetic appeal.

- o **Put to Another Use:** Find alternative applications for a product or idea. *Example*: Bubble wrap, originally wallpaper, became protective packaging.

- o **Eliminate:** Remove unnecessary components to simplify or save costs. *Example*: Removing headphone jacks from phones popularized wireless earbuds.

- o **Reverse:** Rearrange or invert processes to uncover new perspectives. *Example*: IKEA's flat-pack furniture involves customers assembling products, reducing shipping costs.

The founders of Instagram initially created a location-based app called Burbn. After feedback showed users were more interested in the photo-sharing feature, they pivoted by stripping away other functionalities, leading to Instagram's massive success.

Step 3: Evaluate Options and Prioritize

Not all ideas are feasible or impactful. Evaluate solutions based on factors like cost, time, and scalability.

Key Actions:

- Use a decision matrix to rank potential solutions.

- Consider immediate fixes versus long-term strategies.

- Focus on the "80/20 Rule" (Pareto Principle): identify actions that yield the most significant impact with the least effort.

Example:

When faced with production delays, Toyota developed the **Just-In-Time (JIT) system**, prioritizing efficiency by minimizing inventory waste—a decision that revolutionized manufacturing.

Step 4: Implement the Solution

Execution is where ideas come to life. Start small to minimize risk while testing the solution.

Key Actions:

- Create an action plan with clear roles and deadlines.

- Pilot the solution on a smaller scale to gather feedback.

- Monitor progress with measurable KPIs (Key Performance Indicators).

Step 5: Reflect and Iterate

Not every solution will work perfectly on the first attempt. Use setbacks as learning opportunities to refine your approach.

Key Actions:

- Conduct post-implementation reviews. Ask, *"What worked, and what didn't?"*

- Make adjustments based on feedback and results.

- Celebrate small wins to maintain morale and motivation.

"Failure is simply the opportunity to begin again, this time more intelligently." — Henry Ford

The ability to solve problems effectively and cultivate resilience is foundational for entrepreneurial success. By defining challenges, brainstorming innovative solutions, implementing actions, and learning from outcomes, you not only overcome obstacles but also grow stronger. Remember, every problem is an opportunity in disguise, waiting for you to uncover its potential.

Practical Advice for Handling Uncertainty in the Early Stages

Starting a business is exhilarating, but it's also riddled with uncertainty. From securing funding to attracting customers, the early stages of entrepreneurship require resilience, adaptability, and strategic decision-making. Here's practical advice to help navigate uncertainty and build a solid foundation for success:

1. Embrace a Flexible Mindset

Uncertainty is an inherent part of entrepreneurship. A flexible mindset enables you to adapt quickly to changing circumstances.

How to Practice Flexibility:

- **Prepare for Change:** Accept that not everything will go as planned. Create backup plans for critical aspects of your business, like suppliers, funding, or marketing strategies.

- **Adopt Agile Practices:** Break projects into smaller, manageable phases. Evaluate progress regularly and adjust based on feedback.

- **Learn from Setbacks:** View challenges as opportunities for growth and innovation.

When Slack's founders realized their initial gaming project wasn't viable, they pivoted to the internal communication tool they had built for their team. That flexibility turned Slack into a billion-dollar company.

2. Start Small and Test Ideas

Avoid the trap of overcommitting resources to unproven ideas. Begin with minimal viable products (MVPs) and scale based on results.

Steps to Start Small:

1. **Define Your MVP:** Focus on creating a version of your product or service that solves a core customer problem.

2. **Seek Early Feedback:** Share your MVP with a small group of target customers to gather insights.

3. **Iterate Quickly:** Use feedback to refine your offering before investing heavily.

Dropbox launched with a simple demo video showcasing the concept of cloud storage. This low-cost approach validated demand before the product was fully developed.

3. Build a Strong Support Network

Uncertainty feels less daunting when you're surrounded by advisors, mentors, and peers who provide guidance and encouragement.

- **Join Entrepreneurial Communities:** Attend meetups, join online forums, or participate in accelerator programs.

- **Seek Mentorship:** Connect with experienced entrepreneurs who can share insights and help you navigate challenges.

- **Leverage Social Networks:** Platforms like LinkedIn can help you find collaborators, partners, or early adopters.

Example:
Mark Zuckerberg relied on a strong network of advisors, including mentors like Steve Jobs and Don Graham, during Facebook's early days. These connections provided invaluable insights that helped Facebook grow.

4. Manage Finances Conservatively

Financial uncertainty is one of the most significant challenges for startups. Developing a lean approach to spending ensures you can sustain operations during unpredictable times.

Financial Tips:

- Focus on generating revenue early instead of relying solely on external funding.

- Regularly track income and expenses to avoid surprises.

- Set aside reserves to cover at least three to six months of essential expenses.

Sarah Kauss, founder of S'well, self-funded her reusable water bottle business by keeping costs low and reinvesting profits. This lean approach helped her scale sustainably.

5. Focus on What You Can Control

Uncertainty often stems from external factors beyond your influence. Directing your energy toward controllable aspects of your business helps maintain focus and progress.

Practical Actions:

- Improve your product or service.

- Strengthen relationships with customers and partners.

- Enhance your skills or your team's capabilities.

During the COVID-19 pandemic, many restaurants shifted focus from in-house dining to delivery services, concentrating on elements within their control to stay afloat.

6. Communicate Openly and Honestly

Uncertainty can create anxiety for your team and stakeholders. Transparent communication builds trust and fosters collaboration.

Tips for Effective Communication:

- Share your vision and strategy, even if the plan evolves.

- Be honest about challenges and involve your team in finding solutions.

- Regularly update customers about changes or delays.

Tesla faced production delays in its early years. Elon Musk maintained transparency about challenges, which helped retain investor confidence and customer loyalty.

7. Strengthen Emotional Resilience

The emotional toll of uncertainty can lead to burnout if not managed effectively. Resilience allows entrepreneurs to stay motivated during tough times.

Ways to Build Resilience:

- **Practice Self-Care:** Prioritize sleep, nutrition, and exercise.

- **Set Realistic Goals:** Break larger tasks into achievable milestones to reduce overwhelm.

- **Cultivate Optimism:** Focus on progress rather than perfection. Celebrate small wins to maintain morale.

"Resilience is accepting your new reality, even if it's less good than the one you had before." — Elizabeth Edwards

8. Use Data to Reduce Uncertainty

Leverage data to make informed decisions and reduce guesswork. Analytics and customer insights provide clarity in uncertain situations.

Steps to Leverage Data:

- Use tools like Google Analytics or market research platforms to track customer behavior.

- Conduct A/B testing for marketing strategies or product features.

- Regularly review financial reports to identify trends.

Amazon uses customer data extensively to refine its recommendations, ensuring a personalized shopping experience that drives sales.

9. Prepare for Worst-Case Scenarios

Anticipating potential challenges allows you to create contingency plans and remain composed when setbacks occur.

Steps to Prepare:

1. Identify the risks your business faces (e.g., supply chain disruptions, market shifts).

2. Develop action plans for each risk scenario.

3. Regularly revisit and update your contingency plans.

During its expansion, Airbnb faced regulatory challenges in various cities. The company proactively developed legal strategies and adjusted its policies to comply with local laws.

Handling uncertainty in the early stages of entrepreneurship requires a combination of strategic planning, adaptability, and resilience. By staying flexible, focusing on what you can control, and building a robust support system, you can navigate the unknown with confidence. Remember, uncertainty is not your enemy—it's an opportunity to innovate, learn, and grow.

In business, setbacks are not just obstacles; they can be opportunities for growth and success. By adapting, innovating, and staying resilient, you can transform challenges into opportunities that set your business apart.

In the next chapter, *"Stirring the Sweetness,"* I'll explore how to refine your strategies, balance creativity with execution, and maintain consistency in delivering value. Are you ready to take the next step? Let's turn those lemons into something extraordinary.

Chapter 4

Stirring the Sweetness

Business, much like lemonade, thrives on balance. You can gather the best ingredients (vision, resources, and skills) but it's the stirring that blends these components into something extraordinary. Stirring in entrepreneurship means taking action, ensuring consistency, and finding harmony between ambition and practicality. Just as too much sugar can overwhelm a glass of lemonade, excessive ambition without strategy can derail a venture.

In this chapter, we'll explore how to maintain the delicate balance required for entrepreneurial success. From understanding the power of patience and consistency to fostering collaboration, you'll learn strategies to refine your approach and ensure your ideas leave a lasting impression.

Balance in Planning and Execution

Balancing planning and execution are crucial in entrepreneurship, where success relies on both strategy and action. Too much planning without execution can lead to missed opportunities, while hasty actions without a plan often result in inefficiencies and failure. To achieve optimal outcomes, entrepreneurs must strike a balance that leverages the strengths of both.

1. Why Balance Matters

Planning

Planning ensures clarity of objectives, risk management, and effective allocation of resources. According to a Harvard Business School study, poor communication of strategy contributes significantly to organizations failing to meet half their strategic targets. Aligning plans with clear goals helps mitigate this.

Execution

Execution is where ideas meet reality. Even the best strategies falter without proper execution, with research indicating that only a few businesses excel at implementing their strategies. Execution involves implementing plans, gathering feedback, and refining the approach.

Balance

Balancing planning and execution means adapting to changing circumstances while keeping long-term goals in focus. Flexibility in resource allocation, as emphasized by Aaron Hall, enables organizations to remain competitive in dynamic markets.

2. Practical Strategies for Achieving Balance

Clearly define long-term and short-term goals. Involve stakeholders in the planning phase to align vision and resources. Use data-driven insights:

- Leverage analytics to make informed decisions about resource allocation and risk management.

- Advanced tools like KPIs and performance metrics help track progress effectively.

Iterative Approach

Break larger plans into smaller, manageable tasks. Test these tasks, gather feedback, and refine strategies. This approach minimizes risks while ensuring flexibility in execution.

3. Real-Life Examples

Apple's Product Strategy

Apple's balance of long-term planning with flawless execution exemplifies success. Each product launch is meticulously planned yet flexible enough to adapt to market demands. Consistency in quality and messaging underpins its global success.

Netflix's Adaptability

Netflix's transition from DVD rentals to streaming services shows the power of balancing visionary planning with adaptive execution. Recognizing changing consumer behavior, Netflix invested in a streaming platform, leading to industry dominance.

4. Key Takeaways

Ensure every team member understands the objectives. Align planning and execution through clear communication across all levels of the organization. Use measurable KPIs to track and refine strategies and be ready to pivot strategies based on feedback or market changes.

Balancing planning and execution is an art that entrepreneurs must master. By combining clear strategies with decisive actions and remaining adaptable, businesses can thrive even in uncertain conditions. As Dwight Eisenhower aptly said, *"Plans are nothing; planning is everything."* Success lies not in having the perfect plan but in the ability to execute it with discipline and flexibility.

Concept of Patience, Consistency, and Collaboration

In entrepreneurship, success rarely happens overnight. It is built over time through the deliberate application of patience, consistency, and collaboration. These three qualities are essential for sustaining growth, overcoming challenges, and fostering innovation in any venture.

1. Patience

Patience allows entrepreneurs to endure the natural ebb and flow of business, particularly during its early stages. Research according to Cloudvisor, shows that startups typically take 3–5 years to become profitable

During this time, patience enables entrepreneurs to refine their processes, build a customer base, and adapt to unforeseen challenges.

Colonel Harland Sanders of KFC did not achieve success until his 60s. His journey included over 1,000 rejections of his chicken recipe before securing a partnership that made his brand globally recognized. Patience was the cornerstone of his success.

Tips for Practicing Patience

- Understand that building a sustainable business takes time.

- Celebrate Small Wins. Recognize incremental achievements to stay motivated.

- Invest in long-term goals rather than seeking immediate results.

"Great things are not done by impulse, but by a series of small things brought together." — Vincent Van Gogh

2. Consistency

Consistency builds trust among customers, employees, and stakeholders. According to Forbes, companies that consistently deliver high-quality products and services are more likely to retain customers and achieve long-term growth.

Example: Coca-Cola

Coca-Cola's success is rooted in its consistent branding, taste, and marketing over decades. This reliability has fostered customer loyalty and brand recognition globally.

How to Cultivate Consistency

- **Establish Systems:** Create repeatable processes for delivering products or services.

- **Maintain Branding:** Ensure your messaging and visuals align across all platforms.

- **Regularly Evaluate Performance:** Use KPIs to measure consistency in operations and customer satisfaction.

3. Collaboration

Collaboration brings diverse perspectives, skills, and ideas together, fostering innovation and problem-solving. Studies by Frost & Sullivan, indicate that businesses that collaborate are 30% more likely to innovate effectively and at least 36% more productive than those that don't.

Steve Jobs and Steve Wozniak

Apple was born out of the collaboration between Jobs' visionary leadership and Wozniak's technical expertise. Their complementary skills laid the foundation for one of the most innovative companies in history.

Benefits of Collaboration

- A team with varied backgrounds can approach challenges creatively.

- Collaboration distributes responsibilities, preventing burnout.

- Partnerships often open doors to new opportunities and resources.

How to Foster Collaboration

1. Create a culture where ideas are freely shared without fear of judgment.

2. Leverage technology. Use collaborative tools like Slack or Trello to streamline teamwork.

3. Celebrate team successes and individual efforts.

"If you want to go fast, go alone. If you want to go far, go together." — African Proverb

Integrating Patience, Consistency, and Collaboration

Successful entrepreneurs recognize the interplay between these three traits:

- **Patience fuels consistency:** Sticking to processes over time builds reliability.

- **Consistency attracts collaborators:** A track record of dependable performance inspires trust.

- **Collaboration enhances patience:** Working with others provides the support needed to persevere during challenging times.

Practical Exercise:

- Reflect on your current approach to patience, consistency, and collaboration.

- Identify one area where you could improve and create an actionable plan to address it.

Patience, consistency, and collaboration are the heroes of entrepreneurship. Together, they create a foundation for lasting success, enabling entrepreneurs to weather challenges, build trust, and innovate through teamwork. As you integrate these traits into your journey, remember:

that true greatness is built one step at a time, often with the help of others along the way.

Strategies for Young Entrepreneurs to Test and Improve Their Ideas

Testing and refining ideas is a crucial part of the entrepreneurial journey. For young entrepreneurs, starting with practical, cost-effective strategies can provide valuable insights into the viability of their business concepts.

1. Build a Minimum Viable Product (MVP)

An MVP is a basic version of your product or service designed to test its core functionality. This allows you to gather feedback from early adopters without committing excessive resources.

Steps to Create an MVP:

- Identify the primary problem your product solves.
- Focus on essential features.
- Use low-cost methods (e.g., prototypes, mock-ups) to create the MVP.

Dropbox began by sharing a simple demo video to explain its cloud storage concept. This approach validated demand before full-scale development

2. Leverage Social Media Platforms

Social media offers young entrepreneurs a cost-effective way to test ideas and reach potential customers. Polls, surveys, and ads can gauge interest and gather feedback.

How to Use Social Media for Testing:

- Create targeted ads to measure audience interest.

- Post product concepts and ask followers for input.

- Use tools like Instagram Stories polls or LinkedIn feedback threads.

Daniel Wellington successfully tested its minimalist watch designs on Instagram, using influencers to promote prototypes before launching fully.

3. Conduct Focus Groups or Surveys

Engage with a small group of target customers to understand their needs, preferences, and pain points.

Tips for Effective Focus Groups:

- Select participants who represent your ideal customer.

- Ask open-ended questions about your product or service.

- Analyze feedback to identify areas for improvement.

4. Test in Small Markets

Launching your product or service in a smaller, localized market reduces risk while providing actionable insights.

Airbnb initially focused on San Francisco, refining its platform based on user feedback before scaling globally.

5. Embrace Iterative Testing

Use a cycle of trial, feedback, and refinement to continually improve your idea. This iterative process helps identify what works and what needs adjustment.

Steps for Iterative Testing:

- Launch a prototype.

- Collect data from users.

- Analyze the results and adjust accordingly.

Parental Advice: How to Foster a Positive Work Ethic

Parents play a pivotal role in fostering a positive work ethic in their children, leading by example and instilling values like responsibility, perseverance, and collaboration. Children often mirror their parents' attitudes, so demonstrating commitment, punctuality, and resilience in daily tasks creates a strong foundation. Sharing personal challenges and successes can inspire children to adopt a similar mindset, teaching them to embrace effort over immediate results. For instance, praising the time spent improving a school project emphasizes growth and persistence rather than focusing solely on the final grade.

Practical experiences help children internalize the value of hard work. Assign age-appropriate tasks, such as organizing toys for younger children or budgeting for older ones, to teach accountability. Real-world activities like running a lemonade stand or selling crafts give them hands-on experience with effort, planning, and reward.

Encouraging teamwork through family projects or community activities fosters respect for collaboration and demonstrates the importance of shared goals, preparing them for larger challenges in life.

Stories of accomplished figures like Oprah Winfrey and Elon Musk further reinforce the value of a strong work ethic. Sharing how these individuals overcame adversity and succeeded through dedication can serve as powerful inspiration. Parents should highlight that hard work and perseverance often outweigh natural talent, echoing Tim Notke's words: "Hard work beats talent when talent doesn't work hard." By combining real-world guidance with motivational examples, parents can prepare their children for success in life and future careers.

Testing ideas and fostering a strong work ethic are foundational for entrepreneurial success. By employing creative testing strategies, young entrepreneurs can refine their ideas, while parental guidance helps instill the discipline and determination needed to thrive. Together, these strategies build a solid base for future achievements.

Stirring the sweetness in business is an art of balance, patience, and collaboration. By blending these qualities, entrepreneurs can create ventures that not only succeed but also endure. As we move into the next chapter, *"Setting Up Shop,"* I'll explore the practicalities of building your business infrastructure, from branding to operations. So, grab your spoon and keep stirring—the perfect blend is within reach!

Chapter 5

Setting Up Shop

When starting a business, setting up a shop is one of the most significant milestones. It represents the tangible beginning of your entrepreneurial journey and provides the foundation for everything else. Whether your "shop" is a physical storefront, an online marketplace, or even a service-based operation, how you set it up greatly influences your business's success.

This chapter will guide you through the essentials: setting goals, building a brand, choosing platforms, and navigating the legal and logistical considerations. With real-world examples, practical tips, and action steps, you'll learn how to create a strong and enduring foundation for your venture.

Building the Foundation

Setting Goals, Choosing Platforms, and Branding

Building a strong foundation is the first step in transforming a business idea into a reality. It involves clear goal-setting, selecting the right platforms for engagement, and creating a compelling brand identity. These three elements serve as the backbone of any entrepreneurial venture.

1. Defining Your Business Direction

Goals provide clarity, focus, and motivation. They help you define what success looks like and guide your daily activities toward achieving it.

The SMART Framework for Effective Goal Setting:

- **Specific:** Clearly define what you want to achieve.

- **Measurable:** Quantify your progress with metrics.

- **Achievable:** Set realistic and attainable objectives.

- **Relevant:** Align goals with your broader business vision.

- **Time-bound:** Establish a deadline to create urgency.

Example Goal for a Lemonade Stand: *Sell 500 cups of lemonade within three months while maintaining a 30% profit margin.*

Actionable Steps to Set Goals:

1. Write down your business's long-term vision.

2. Break it into smaller, actionable steps.

3. Track progress regularly to stay on course.

"Setting goals is the first step in turning the invisible into the visible." — Tony Robbins

2. Where and How to Engage Customers

Physical or Digital Platforms: The choice between a physical or digital platform depends on the nature of your business, target audience, and available resources.

Physical Platforms:

- **Location Matters:** For a physical business, choose high-traffic areas accessible to your target audience.

- **Examples:** Busy street corners, local farmers' markets, or community events.

Digital Platforms:

An online presence is vital for reaching a broader audience.

- **Website:** Platforms like Wix or Shopify simplify creating a user-friendly and professional site.

- **Social Media:** Choose platforms where your audience is active (e.g., Instagram for young audiences or LinkedIn for professionals).

- **E-commerce:** For selling products, leverage platforms like Etsy, Amazon, or your website.

Pro Tip: Optimize your online presence for mobile devices, according to *Go-Globe*, over 54% of web traffic comes from smartphones. Warby Parker started as an online-only retailer, leveraging its e-commerce platform to test demand before expanding to physical stores.

3. Shaping Your Business Identity

Branding creates an emotional connection with customers, sets you apart from competitors, and fosters loyalty. It's more than just a logo—it's how your business is perceived.

Steps to Build a Strong Brand:

1. **Define Your Mission and Values:**

   o What does your business stand for?

   o How do you want customers to feel when interacting with your brand?

2. **Create a Visual Identity:**

   o Design a memorable logo and choose consistent fonts and colors.

   o Use tools like Canva for affordable and professional designs.

3. **Develop a Unique Voice:**

   o Craft messaging that reflects your values and resonates with your audience.

   o Maintain a consistent tone across all communication channels.

4. **Promote Your Brand:**

   o **Word-of-Mouth:** Encourage satisfied customers to share their experiences. Offer incentives like discounts for referrals to encourage happy customers to promote your business.

- o **Social Media:** Use platforms like Instagram, TikTok, or LinkedIn to connect with customers and showcase your products. Share behind-the-scenes content, customer testimonials, and promotions.

- o **Traditional Advertising:** Distribute flyers, use local radio spots, or participate in community events.

Example for a Lemonade Stand: Brand your lemonade stand as "Sunshine Sips," with a cheerful yellow logo, friendly messaging, and a social media campaign sharing customer reviews. "Your brand is what people say about you when you're not in the room." — Jeff Bezos

4. Pricing Strategy

Your pricing strategy significantly impacts customer perception and profitability. It's about finding a balance between affordability and profitability while aligning with your brand positioning.

1. **Understand Your Costs:**

   - o Calculate the cost of goods sold (COGS) and factor in operational expenses.

   - o Don't forget hidden costs like marketing, packaging, or delivery.

2. **Know Your Market:** Research competitors' pricing to ensure you remain competitive while highlighting your unique value.

3. **Adopt a Psychological Pricing Model:**

   o Use prices that end in .99 to create the perception of affordability (e.g., $4.99).

   o Bundle products to offer perceived value (e.g., buy two, get one free).

4. **Dynamic Pricing:** Adjust your prices based on demand, seasons, or special events. For example, during hot summer days, a lemonade stand can charge a premium.

5. Customer Service

Exceptional customer service transforms first-time buyers into loyal advocates. It's an extension of your brand and shapes the customer experience.

1. **Train for Excellence:**

   o Teach employees to greet customers warmly, listen actively, and address complaints professionally.

   o Equip staff with the knowledge to answer questions confidently.

2. **Personalize the Experience:**

   o Use customer names, remember preferences, and follow up to show care and attention.

    ○ Leverage CRM tools to manage customer relationships effectively.

3. **Respond Promptly:** Quick responses to inquiries or complaints, especially on social media, demonstrate attentiveness.

4. **Gather Feedback:** Use surveys, suggestion boxes, or follow-up emails to understand customer needs and refine your service.

Checklist for Building a Strong Foundation

- Have you set clear and measurable business goals?

- Is your platform (physical or digital) optimized for accessibility and customer engagement?

- Does your branding reflect your mission and resonate with your target audience?

- Are your promotional strategies (word-of-mouth, social media, advertising) aligned with your goals?

Building the foundation for your business is about creating a roadmap, choosing the right tools, and crafting an identity that connects with customers. As you lay the groundwork, remember that a strong start sets the stage for enduring success.

Tips on Creating a Workspace or Online Presence

Creating a Physical Workspace

1. **Optimize for Productivity:**

   o Choose a clutter-free area with minimal distractions.

   o Use ergonomic furniture to promote comfort and reduce strain during long hours.

2. **Add Personal Touches:**

   o Decorate with motivational quotes, a vision board, or your brand colors.

   o Incorporate natural lighting and greenery to improve mood and focus.

3. **Ensure Accessibility:**

   o For physical shops, ensure the location is easy to find and accessible to your target customers.

   o Pay attention to parking, foot traffic, and nearby businesses that may complement yours.

Example:

A teenager running a custom jewelry business could set up a small workspace at home with organized trays for materials and a photography corner for product images.

Online Presence Tips:

- **Start with a Website:** Use platforms like Wix or Shopify for user-friendly website creation.

- **Engage on Social Media:** Post regular updates and interact with followers on platforms like Instagram, Facebook, and LinkedIn.

- **Optimize for SEO:** Use keywords to improve your website's visibility on search engines.

The Significance of a Strong Support System

No entrepreneur succeeds alone. Having a support system of mentors, peers, friends, and family can make a tremendous difference.

Benefits of a Support System:

Mentors:

- Provide expertise, constructive feedback, and advice based on experience.

- Help navigate complex decisions and avoid common pitfalls.

Example:
Many successful entrepreneurs, like Mark Zuckerberg, attribute their early success to mentorship from experienced professionals like Steve Jobs.

Parents:

- Offer emotional and sometimes financial support.

- Help foster confidence and resilience by encouraging learning through trial and error.

Activity for Parents: Encourage your child by attending their first trade show or sharing their business on social media.

Friends:

- Act as cheerleaders, spreading word-of-mouth referrals.

- Collaborate or contribute to brainstorming sessions with fresh perspectives.

"If you want to go fast, go alone. If you want to go far, go together." — African Proverb

Legal and Logistical Considerations Simplified

Starting a business involves navigating some essential legal and logistical steps.

Legal Requirements:

- **Register Your Business:** Choose a business structure (e.g., sole proprietorship, LLC) and register with local authorities.

- **Get Permits and Licenses:** Research any necessary permits for your location and industry.

- **Understand Tax Obligations:** Ensure compliance with tax regulations to avoid penalties.

The U.S. Small Business Administration provides detailed guides on legal requirements for new businesses. You can visit their website for more details: https://www.sba.gov/federal-contracting/contracting-guide/basic-requirements

Logistical Setup:

- **Supplies and Inventory:** Source quality materials and maintain adequate stock.

- **Payment Systems:** Use reliable tools like Square or PayPal for seamless transactions.

- **Insurance:** Protect your business with liability and property insurance.

Example:
Shopify offers integrated tools for inventory management, shipping, and payment processing, simplifying logistics for e-commerce entrepreneurs.

Reflective Exercises and Checklists

1. **Goal-Setting Exercise:** Write down your long-term vision and break it into short-term actionable steps.

2. **Workspace Checklist:**

   o Is your workspace safe and functional?

   o Do you have the tools you need to operate efficiently?

3. **Support System Map:** Identify mentors, peers, and family members who can support you, and reach out to them.

Setting up shop is more than just opening a door or launching a website—it's about creating a strong foundation for success. From defining your goals and branding to securing a support system and handling legal requirements, each step is vital.

As you embark on this exciting phase, remember that preparation and execution go hand in hand. In the next chapter, *"The First Pour,"* we'll dive into the launch phase and explore how to make a strong initial impression. Your shop is ready—let's open it with a splash!

Chapter 6

The First Pour

There's nothing quite like the exhilaration of launching your first product or idea. It's that defining moment when dreams turn into reality. For young entrepreneurs, this is a mix of excitement and fear—the "first pour." Imagine the rush of pouring that first glass of lemonade at your stand or receiving your first online order. It's thrilling, nerve-wracking, and utterly rewarding. This chapter explores how to navigate this monumental milestone, turning jitters into joy and potential into success.

The Excitement and Fear of Launching a Product or Idea

Launching a product or idea is often accompanied by a blend of excitement and fear. It's a transformative moment that validates your hard work and ideas, but it also introduces uncertainty. This section explores strategies to harness excitement, manage fear, and confidently step into the entrepreneurial world.

The Excitement of Launching

Excitement drives energy, creativity, and enthusiasm. It reflects your passion and is contagious. Customers and stakeholders are more likely to engage with a business driven by visible enthusiasm. When Steve Jobs introduced the first iPhone, his excitement was palpable. His passion for the product's potential captivated audiences and set the stage for its monumental success.

How to Harness Excitement:

1. **Channel Energy into Preparation:** Use your excitement to fine-tune your product and plan a memorable launch. Create marketing campaigns that reflect your passion.

2. **Celebrate Progress:** Acknowledge the work that got you to this point. Share your journey with your audience to build a deeper connection.

3. **Visualize Success:** Imagine your product resonating with customers. Visualization can boost confidence and maintain focus on your goals.

"Enthusiasm moves the world." — Arthur Balfour

The Fear of Launching

Understanding Fear

Fear often stems from uncertainty and concerns about how the product will be received, whether customers will engage, or if the effort will pay off. However, fear is also a sign of growth, pushing you outside your comfort zone.

Common Fears Among Entrepreneurs:

- Fear of failure or rejection.

- Financial insecurity.

- Negative feedback from customers or peers.

Strategies to Manage Fear

1. Reframe Fear as Excitement

Forbes's publication confirmed that physiological responses to fear and excitement are similar to heart racing, increased focus, and adrenaline. Shift your mindset by telling yourself, *"I'm excited!"* rather than, *"I'm scared."*

Tip:
Practice mindfulness and affirmations such as, *"This is my opportunity to grow and succeed."*

2. Prepare Thoroughly

Preparation reduces uncertainty and builds confidence. The more you understand your product, audience, and market, the less intimidating the launch becomes.

Checklist:
- Have you tested your product with a pilot audience?
- Do you have a clear marketing and sales strategy?
- Have you anticipated and addressed potential risks?

The founders of Airbnb prepared extensively before their official launch, refining their platform based on user feedback during their early trials.

3. Focus on Your Why

Reconnect with your purpose. Why did you start this journey? Grounding yourself in your mission can help you overcome fears.

Exercise:

Write a short paragraph about why your product matters and revisit it whenever self-doubt creeps in.

4. Start Small

This can't be overemphasized, launching doesn't have to be grandiose. Starting small allows you to test your product, gather feedback, and build momentum without overwhelming pressure.

5. Accept Imperfection

No product or launch is perfect. Embrace the idea of learning from mistakes and adapting as you go. "Done is better than perfect." —Sheryl Sandberg

Balancing Excitement and Fear

1. **Reflect on Your Journey:** Use excitement to appreciate how far you've come. Channel fear into motivation for improvement.

2. **Engage Your Support System:** Share your feelings with mentors, family, or friends. Their encouragement can help you maintain perspective.

3. **Practice Mindfulness:** Techniques like deep breathing or meditation can calm your mind and keep you grounded.

The duality of excitement and fear is a natural part of launching any product or idea. While excitement fuels passion and creativity, fear can serve as a guide to areas needing attention. Embrace both emotions, prepare thoroughly, and take the leap with confidence. Remember, every successful business began with a single step—this is yours!

First Sale Tips

Customer Interaction, Feedback, and Building Confidence

The first sale is a defining moment for any entrepreneur. It's not just about the transaction—it's about learning, connecting, and setting a strong foundation for future growth. Here's how to make your first sale count:

1. Customer Interaction: Making a Memorable First Impression

Customer interaction sets the tone for your business. Greet your first customers warmly and authentically. Show genuine interest in their needs by asking open-ended questions such as, *"What made you interested in our product?"* Tailoring your conversation to their responses makes them feel valued.

Pro Tip: Maintain eye contact, smile, and thank customers personally. These small gestures can leave a lasting positive impression.

2. Feedback: A Tool for Growth

Your first customers are invaluable sources of insight. Encourage feedback by asking for their thoughts on the product and overall experience. Use simple surveys or ask informal questions like, *"What did you enjoy most, and is there anything we could improve?"*

Feedback helps refine your offering and shows customers that their opinions matter. Sharing your commitment to improvement can foster loyalty.

Early users of Instagram provided feedback on filters and usability, helping the team enhance the app before scaling it globally.

3. Building Confidence Through Experience

Confidence grows with practice. Prepare for your first sale by rehearsing your pitch, familiarizing yourself with your product, and planning for potential questions. If things don't go perfectly, focus on what you can learn and improve.

Exercise: After your first sale, reflect on what went well and what could be better. Write these down to build confidence for future interactions. "Confidence is preparation. Everything else is beyond your control." — Richard Kline

By focusing on authentic customer interactions, valuing feedback, and embracing growth, your first sale can be more than a transaction—it can be the foundation of a thriving business.

Celebrate Small wins

In the entrepreneurial journey, small wins are more than milestones—they're motivators. Celebrating these achievements reinforces progress, builds momentum, and cultivates a positive mindset.

Each step forward, no matter how minor, reflects your growth and hard work. Celebrating these moments boosts morale and creates a sense of accomplishment. Research from the Harvard Business Review highlights how acknowledging progress improves motivation and productivity.

If your business sells five products in its first week, celebrate! It's proof that your efforts are resonating with customers. Creative ways to celebrate small wins are:

- **Personal Rewards:** Treat yourself to something meaningful, like a favorite meal or an afternoon off.

- **Team Celebrations:** If you work with a team, acknowledge everyone's contributions with a small gathering or public praise.

- **Share with Your Community:** Announce your milestones on social media. Customers love to see the businesses they support succeed.

Tip: Keep a "win journal" where you jot down achievements, big or small. Revisiting these entries during challenging times can reignite your motivation.

Each victory is a stepping stone toward larger goals. Use small successes to reflect on strategies that worked and replicate them on a bigger scale. "Success is the sum of small efforts, repeated day in and day out." — Robert Collier

Celebrating small wins not only recognizes effort but also keeps the entrepreneurial spirit alive. These moments remind you why you started and inspire you to continue moving forward.

Role of Parents as Cheerleaders and Constructive Critics

Parents play a unique and essential role in fostering a child's entrepreneurial spirit. Their support can shape confidence, resilience, and decision-making skills, turning dreams into actionable ventures.

1. Providing Unwavering Encouragement

Parents' encouragement motivates young entrepreneurs to believe in their ideas. Celebrate milestones with them, attend their first events, and share their achievements with friends and family. A positive environment cultivates self-assurance.

Parents can share their child's first success on social media, helping them attract more customers. Simple acts like these show enthusiasm and amplify visibility.

2. Constructive Critics

While cheerleading is important, constructive criticism ensures children learn and grow. Instead of focusing on mistakes, highlight areas of improvement with actionable suggestions.

How to Be Constructive:

- **Be Specific:** Instead of saying, *"This didn't work,"* try, *"Your sign could be clearer to attract more customers."*

- **Balance Feedback:** Pair critique with praise to maintain confidence.

Tip: Use a "feedback sandwich" approach—start with a positive, provide constructive advice, and end with encouragement.

3. Teaching Resilience and Accountability

Entrepreneurship isn't just about success; it's about learning to handle setbacks. Parents can share stories of challenges they've faced and how they overcame them, demonstrating resilience.

Activity for Parents: Encourage children to reflect on challenges and identify lessons learned. Guide them in finding solutions rather than offering immediate fixes.

By being both cheerleaders and constructive critics, parents provide the foundation for young entrepreneurs to thrive. Their involvement fosters confidence, encourages reflection, and instills life-long problem-solving skills.

Reflective Exercises and Action Plans

1. **Sales Reflection Journal:**

   - After your first sale, jot down what went well and what you'd improve.

   - Use this reflection to prepare for your next sale.

2. **Feedback Analysis:**

   - Collect feedback from your first customers.

   - Identify common themes and adjust your strategy accordingly.

3. **Celebration Tracker:**

- ○ Create a list of milestones (e.g., first sale, first five-star review).

- ○ Plan small celebrations for each achievement.

The first pour represents more than just a sale—it's a declaration of belief in yourself and your idea. Celebrate the excitement, embrace the nerves, and use every interaction as a learning opportunity. With each pour, you're not just building a business; you're crafting a story of persistence, passion, and purpose.

In the next chapter, *"Making Lemonade from Lemons,"* I'll explore how to navigate setbacks and turn challenges into opportunities. Remember, every great business starts with a single pour—make yours count!

Chapter 7

Making Lemonade from Lemons

In the entrepreneurial journey, setbacks are inevitable. Just as lemons are sour by nature, challenges in business can feel disheartening. But within every challenge lies an opportunity. "Making lemonade from lemons" isn't just a cliché—it's a metaphor for resilience, adaptability, and creativity. This chapter explores practical ways to pivot when plans go awry, showcases inspiring stories of entrepreneurs who thrived after failure, and offers actionable exercises for identifying alternative paths to success. For parents, we also delve into how to instill resilience and positivity in young entrepreneurs.

Practical Advice on Pivoting When Plans Don't Work

Successful entrepreneurs know how to pivot—adjusting their strategy while staying aligned with their core vision. Here's how you can effectively pivot when plans don't work.

1. Acknowledge the Setback and Stay Calm

When plans go awry, it's natural to feel overwhelmed or discouraged. However, the first step to pivoting is to accept the situation without panic. Acknowledging the setback allows you to focus on solutions rather than dwelling on the problem.

2. Assess the Situation Objectively

Take a step back and analyze why the plan didn't work. Was it due to external factors like market trends or internal misalignment, such as pricing or product features? Use tools like SWOT analysis (Strengths, Weaknesses, Opportunities, Threats) to identify areas for improvement.

Questions to Ask:

- What specific factors contributed to the failure?

- Are there external forces (e.g., economic conditions) influencing the outcome?

- Are there hidden strengths or opportunities in the current situation?

3. Refocus on Your Core Vision

A pivot doesn't mean abandoning your original goals. Instead, it's about finding a new path that aligns with your overall mission. Reassess what your business stands for and how you can achieve your vision in a different way.

4. Engage with Your Customers

Your customers are a valuable source of insight. Use surveys, focus groups, or direct conversations to understand their needs and expectations. Often, a pivot arises from better aligning your offerings with customer desires.

Pro Tip: Leverage social media to ask customers for feedback. Tools like Instagram polls or Twitter threads can generate quick, actionable responses.

5. Experiment with Small Changes

Pivoting doesn't have to be drastic. Start with incremental adjustments and measure their impact. This approach minimizes risk while allowing you to test what works.

Netflix transitioned from DVD rentals to streaming by first testing the streaming service alongside their original model. The data showed that streaming had higher growth potential, leading to the full pivot.

6. Communicate the Pivot Clearly

If your pivot impacts stakeholders, such as customers, employees, or investors, communicate the reasons behind the change transparently. Highlight the benefits of the new direction and reassure them of your commitment to delivering value. When Airbnb pivoted from offering shared spaces to entire home rentals, they communicated this shift as a way to provide more personalized and flexible options for travelers.

7. Leverage Technology and Innovation

Use digital tools to streamline the pivot process. For example:

- Use analytics to track customer behavior and identify new opportunities.

- Employ project management tools like Trello or Asana to organize tasks.

- Implement marketing automation platforms to test new messaging.

Exercise

1. Write down a recent setback in your business.

2. Answer these questions:

   o What went wrong?

   o What aspects of your business still show promise?

   o What adjustments can you make to better meet customer needs?

Pivoting is not a sign of failure; it's a testament to your adaptability and commitment to success. Whether you're altering your product, strategy, or market focus, the key is to stay true to your vision while embracing change. With resilience, creativity, and a customer-centric approach, you can transform setbacks into opportunities for growth.

Stories of Entrepreneurs Who Succeeded After Failure

Here's a list of inspiring stories of entrepreneurs who found massive success after overcoming failure:

1. J.K. Rowling – Harry Potter Franchise

Before Harry Potter became a global phenomenon, Rowling faced multiple rejections from publishers, lived on welfare, and struggled as a single mother. Her perseverance paid off with one of the best-selling book series in history.

2. Walt Disney – The Walt Disney Company

Disney was fired from a newspaper for "lacking creativity." He faced bankruptcy and business failures before launching Disney Studios, which became the foundation of a global entertainment empire.

3. Oprah Winfrey – OWN Network

Oprah faced numerous professional setbacks, including being demoted from her first job as a TV news anchor. Her determination led to her rise as a talk show host and media mogul.

4. Colonel Harland Sanders – KFC

At age 65, Sanders faced rejection over 1,000 times before finding success with his fried chicken recipe, which became the foundation of KFC.

5. Elon Musk – Tesla and SpaceX

Musk faced near bankruptcy with both Tesla and SpaceX. SpaceX's early launches failed, but his relentless pursuit of innovation turned both companies into industry leaders.

6. Henry Ford – Ford Motor Company

Ford went bankrupt twice before succeeding with the Ford Motor Company, revolutionizing the auto industry with assembly line production.

7. Arianna Huffington – The Huffington Post

Huffington's second book was rejected by 36 publishers. Later, she launched The Huffington Post, which became a widely read and influential media platform.

8. Milton Hershey – Hershey's

Before founding the Hershey Company, Milton Hershey started and failed with three candy businesses. His persistence eventually led to the creation of the iconic Hershey's chocolate brand.

9. Vera Wang – Fashion Designer

Wang was rejected from the U.S. Olympic figure skating team and faced setbacks as a journalist. Pivoting to fashion, she became one of the most recognized designers in bridal wear.

10. Richard Branson – Virgin Group

Branson faced several business failures, including the collapse of Virgin Cola and Virgin Brides. Nevertheless, his willingness to take risks paid off and Virgin became a global brand.

11. Soichiro Honda – Honda

Honda was turned down by Toyota for a job as an engineer and later faced multiple setbacks with his company. His persistence eventually made Honda a leading name in the automotive and motorcycle industries.

12. Mark Cuban – Billionaire Investor

Cuban was fired from several jobs, including one at a computer store, before starting MicroSolutions, which he later sold for millions. His entrepreneurial journey eventually made him a billionaire.

13. Barbara Corcoran – Real Estate Mogul

Before becoming a star on *Shark Tank*, Corcoran failed at several ventures and even faced betrayal from a business partner. She built a multi-million-dollar real estate business against the odds.

14. Fred Smith – FedEx

Smith's college professor said his concept for a logistics company would never work. After launching FedEx, he faced financial difficulties but persevered, creating a global shipping giant.

These stories remind us that failure is often a stepping stone to success. Which one resonates most with you?

Exercises for Identifying Alternative Paths to Success

1. SWOT Analysis with a Twist

A traditional SWOT (Strengths, Weaknesses, Opportunities, Threats) analysis is a powerful tool for assessing your current situation. Add a creative element by focusing on how your weaknesses and threats can be turned into strengths and opportunities.

A young entrepreneur running a lemonade stand might identify:

- **Strength:** Unique flavors.

- **Weakness:** Limited marketing budget.

- **Opportunity:** High local demand for organic drinks.

- **Threat:** Competing stands in the area.

Steps:

1. Write down your business's current strengths, weaknesses, opportunities, and threats.

2. For each weakness, brainstorm one way to overcome or mitigate it.

3. For each threat, identify a strategy to turn it into an opportunity.

If high competition is a threat, consider how your unique branding or customer service could stand out in the market.

2. Reverse Brainstorming

Instead of thinking about how to succeed, ask yourself how you might fail. This technique allows you to identify vulnerabilities and develop strategies to avoid pitfalls.

Steps:

1. Write down all the ways your business could fail.

2. Analyze these potential failures and brainstorm solutions to counteract them.

3. Implement safeguards to prevent these scenarios.

Tip:
This exercise helps you proactively address challenges before they arise.

3. Customer Feedback Mapping

Your customers are often the best source of insight for alternative paths. Use their feedback to guide your decisions.

Steps:

1. Collect feedback through surveys, interviews, or social media interactions.

2. Categorize feedback into themes (e.g., product improvements, pricing concerns, service suggestions).

3. Create a map of actionable changes based on recurring feedback.

Example:
A small bakery receiving frequent requests for gluten-free products could introduce a dedicated line to attract a new customer base.

4. Role-Reversal Problem Solving

Put yourself in the shoes of different stakeholders—customers, competitors, or employees—to see your business from their perspectives.

Steps:

1. Ask, "If I were a customer, what would I want to see improved?"

2. Consider, "If I were a competitor, how would I capitalize on this market?"

3. Identify changes based on these insights and prioritize actions.

Tip:
Thinking like a competitor can help you spot untapped opportunities and weaknesses in your strategy.

5. Mind Mapping for Innovation

Visualizing your thoughts can unlock creative solutions. Mind mapping encourages nonlinear thinking and helps connect ideas.

Steps:

1. Write your business challenge in the center of a blank page.

2. Draw branches for possible solutions, related ideas, and potential outcomes.

3. Expand each branch until you've explored all possible paths.

Example:
If a product isn't selling well, a mind map might reveal alternative marketing strategies, product variations, or new target audiences.

6. Scenario Planning

Imagine several future scenarios and develop strategies for each one. This approach prepares you for a range of possibilities and ensures flexibility.

Steps:

1. Identify three scenarios: optimistic, realistic, and pessimistic outcomes.

2. For each scenario, outline actionable steps to adapt and thrive.

3. Monitor market trends to adjust your approach as needed.

During the pandemic, many restaurants created scenarios for reopening, delivery-only services, and online cooking classes, allowing them to pivot quickly as circumstances changed.

7. Reflection Journaling

Reflecting on past challenges and successes can help you identify patterns and potential solutions.

Prompt Questions:

- What challenges have I overcome before, and how did I do it?

- Are there strategies I haven't tried that align with my skills or resources?

- What is one unconventional idea I could pursue today?

8. Innovation Partnerships

Collaborating with others often sparks ideas you wouldn't have thought of alone.

Steps:

1. Reach out to complementary businesses or mentors for brainstorming sessions.

2. Share challenges openly and ask for feedback.

3. Explore partnerships that leverage both parties' strengths.

Example:

A local fitness studio might partner with a nutritionist to offer wellness packages, tapping into a broader customer base.

Exploring alternative paths to success requires a mix of creativity, strategic thinking, and input from others. By practicing these exercises, you'll cultivate a mindset that turns challenges into opportunities, ensuring that your entrepreneurial journey stays dynamic and adaptable. Always remember: the path to success is rarely a straight line—it's the detours that often lead to greatness.

Making lemonade from lemons is about more than just overcoming obstacles—it's about thriving because of them. By pivoting, staying creative, and embracing resilience, you can turn setbacks into stepping stones for success. For parents, teaching these skills ensures the next generation of entrepreneurs is ready to tackle life's challenges with positivity and determination.

In the next chapter, *"Leaving a Legacy,"* I'll explore how to create a lasting impact through your entrepreneurial journey. The lemonade stand isn't just a business; it's a foundation for something far greater. Stay tuned!

Chapter 8

Leaving a Legacy

Business success is commonly measured by profits and market influence. Yet, the most enduring measure of success lies in the legacy we leave behind which involves a positive, lasting impact on people, communities, and industries. Leaving a legacy means crafting something greater than oneself, something that inspires others, empowers communities, and fosters growth long after we are gone. This chapter will teach you the profound importance of creating a meaningful legacy and explore actionable ways entrepreneurs can leave their mark.

The Importance of Creating Impact and Inspiring Others

Businesses today are increasingly judged not just by the numbers on their balance sheets but by the positive impact they create. Going beyond profits allows entrepreneurs to craft legacies that inspire, uplift, and create long-lasting value for people and communities. Here's why and how focusing on impact and inspiration can elevate your business.

1. Building Trust and Loyalty

Modern consumers are drawn to businesses that stand for something more than profit. According to a 2023 study by Nielsen, 73% of global consumers prefer to purchase from brands that prioritize social responsibility and sustainability.

TOMS revolutionized the concept of business impact with its "One for One" model, donating a pair of shoes for every pair sold. This initiative not only met a tangible need but also turned customers into advocates for the brand.

2. Creating Value for Communities

Businesses can strengthen communities by addressing local or global challenges. Whether it's through fair labor practices, environmental stewardship, or community outreach, impactful businesses create ecosystems of growth and development.

Unilever's "Sustainable Living Plan" focuses on reducing environmental impact while improving the health and well-being of 1 billion people. This dual focus on profit and purpose has driven long-term success and inspired industry peers.

3. Inspiring Future Entrepreneurs

When businesses prioritize impact, they inspire others to follow suit. By leading with purpose, entrepreneurs create a ripple effect that encourages employees, customers, and peers to contribute meaningfully to society.

Elon Musk's ventures—Tesla and SpaceX—are rooted in the mission to accelerate sustainable energy and explore interplanetary life, respectively. These bold visions inspire countless individuals to think beyond conventional boundaries.

4. Fostering Employee Engagement

Purpose-driven companies see higher levels of employee satisfaction and productivity. When employees feel their work contributes to a greater cause, they become more invested in their roles.

Tip for Entrepreneurs: Share your company's purpose and goals regularly with your team. Encourage their involvement in creating impact-driven initiatives.

5. Integrating Social Responsibility

Social responsibility should not be an afterthought but an integral part of your business strategy. Identify causes that align with your brand values and core operations.

Ben & Jerry's embeds social and environmental initiatives into every facet of its operations, from sourcing fair-trade ingredients to advocating for racial and climate justice.

Set measurable goals to track your progress in creating positive change. Use metrics like the Social Return on Investment (SROI) to evaluate how your efforts benefit stakeholders beyond your shareholders.

Identify three ways your business can contribute to its community. Set specific, actionable goals for each initiative, and monitor their outcomes.

6. Storytelling: Amplifying Your Impact

Sharing your journey of impact can inspire others and build your brand. Use platforms like blogs, social media, and public speaking engagements to tell your story.

The "Buy a Lady a Drink" campaign by Stella Artois and Water.org shares stories of how access to clean water changes lives, creating an emotional connection with customers and driving global awareness.

7. Financial Benefits of Impact

Impact-driven businesses benefit the world and improve financial performance. Companies that integrate purpose into their operations often see increased customer loyalty, employee retention, and market differentiation.

"Doing well by doing good is no longer just a saying—it's a business imperative." — Howard Schultz, former CEO of Starbucks

Going beyond profits to create impact and inspire others is not a lofty ideal but a powerful strategy for building lasting value. By addressing societal challenges, engaging employees, and sharing your vision, you can build a business that stands out in the market and in the hearts of those it touches. Remember, the legacy of an entrepreneur isn't just measured in dollars—it's reflected in the positive difference they make in the world.

Mentorship, Sharing Knowledge and Giving Back to the Community

Mentorship, sharing knowledge, and giving back to the community are cornerstones of leaving a lasting entrepreneurial legacy. These actions enrich the lives of others and also solidify the impact of your work, ensuring that your vision and values extend far beyond your immediate success.

1. The Power of Mentorship

Why Mentorship Matters: Mentorship is a transformative relationship where experienced entrepreneurs guide the next generation. It provides mentees with invaluable insights, reduces their learning curve, and equips them with the confidence to navigate challenges.

Oprah Winfrey credits mentorship from Maya Angelou as a critical influence in her life. This guidance helped Oprah shape her vision for impactful storytelling and philanthropy.

How to Be an Effective Mentor:

1. **Offer Practical Insights:** Share real-world experiences and actionable advice tailored to the mentee's goals.

2. **Listen and Encourage:** Provide a safe space for mentees to express concerns and explore ideas.

3. **Set Clear Goals:** Work with your mentee to define objectives and create a roadmap for achieving them.

Benefits of Mentorship for Mentors:

- Deepen your understanding of your field through teaching.

- Strengthen your professional network.

- Solidify your own legacy by contributing to others' success.

2. Sharing Knowledge for Collective Growth

Why Share Knowledge? Entrepreneurial knowledge has the power to uplift entire industries and communities. When you share your expertise, you empower others to innovate, adapt, and thrive.

Ways to Share Knowledge:

- **Workshops and Webinars:** Host educational sessions to teach skills, strategies, or emerging trends.

- **Books and Articles:** Document your journey and insights for a wider audience.

- **Public Speaking:** Use conferences and events to inspire and educate a broader community.

Bill Gates' public sharing of insights through his foundation, books, and talks has educated millions on global health and technology, amplifying his impact far beyond his business ventures.

3. Giving Back to the Community

The Role of Social Responsibility: Businesses that invest in their communities foster goodwill, trust, and long-term growth. Giving back can take many forms, such as financial support, volunteering, or advocacy.

Practical Ideas for Giving Back:

1. **Local Initiatives:** Support schools, small businesses, or community projects in your area.

2. **Sustainable Practices:** Implement environmentally friendly policies that benefit both the planet and your stakeholders.

3. **Philanthropy:** Donate a portion of profits to causes aligned with your brand values.

Salesforce's 1-1-1 model donates 1% of its equity, product, and employee time to communities in need, showcasing how corporate giving can be seamlessly integrated into a business model.

Tips for Documenting Success Stories for Future Generations

Documenting your entrepreneurial journey ensures that your lessons, innovations, and values endure. Here's how to preserve and share your story effectively:

1. Keep a Business Journal

Regularly record milestones, challenges, and achievements. Over time, these entries will create a rich tapestry of your journey.

What to Include:

- Key decisions and their outcomes.
- Lessons learned from successes and failures.
- Reflections on your mission and values.

2. Create Digital Content

Use modern tools to share your story with a global audience. Blogs, podcasts, and videos are accessible ways to reach and inspire future generations.

Simon Sinek's viral TED Talk, *Start With Why,* not only documented his philosophy but also became a global movement for purpose-driven leadership.

3. Write a Book or Memoir

Publishing a book consolidates your experiences and insights into a timeless resource. Highlight pivotal moments, strategies, and the values that guided your journey.

Pro Tip: Incorporate personal anecdotes and lessons to make your story relatable and engaging.

4. Leverage Social Media

Platforms like LinkedIn, Instagram, and YouTube allow you to share bite-sized stories and updates in real-time. Use hashtags and geotags to reach relevant audiences.

Tip:
Create a content calendar to maintain consistency and showcase diverse aspects of your journey, from behind-the-scenes glimpses to community outreach efforts.

5. Collaborate with Media Outlets

Partner with journalists, bloggers, or documentary filmmakers to capture and share your story. External perspectives can add depth and authenticity to your narrative.

Elon Musk's interviews and features in major publications document not only his ventures but also his vision for the future, inspiring countless aspiring entrepreneurs.

Mentorship, sharing knowledge, and giving back to the community are not just acts of generosity—they are essential steps toward creating a legacy. By documenting your journey and sharing your insights, you ensure that your story continues to inspire and guide future generations. Remember, the true measure of success lies not in what you achieve but in how your achievements empower others.

Leaving a legacy is about more than making a profit—it's about creating value that lasts. Whether through mentorship, community impact, or inspiring future generations, the true mark of entrepreneurial success lies in the difference you make. By fostering a culture of excellence, sharing knowledge, and aligning actions with purpose, your business can leave an indelible mark on the world.

In the final chapter, "Conclusion," I'll tie together the lessons from this journey, encouraging you to take actionable steps toward turning your entrepreneurial dreams into a lasting legacy. Stay inspired, and let's shape a future worth remembering!

Chapter 9

Conclusion

The entrepreneurial journey is one of creativity, resilience, and growth—a path paved with lessons learned from triumphs and trials. In this book, *Lemonade for Sale: A Guide to Nurturing the Spirit of Entrepreneurship*, we've used the simple yet powerful metaphor of a lemonade stand to explore the essence of building a business from the ground up. As we conclude, let us reflect on the invaluable lessons gleaned from this journey and explore how they empower us to create legacies beyond mere profit.

A Recap of Key Lessons

The lemonade stand serves as a symbol of entrepreneurial spirit—starting small, thinking big, and turning simple ideas into impactful ventures. This metaphor has illuminated core principles:

Every business begins with identifying a niche and crafting a unique selling proposition (USP). Whether it's offering the freshest lemonade on a summer day or introducing a disruptive technology, success stems from knowing your value and articulating it clearly.

Much like crafting the perfect lemonade, entrepreneurship is about balance—mixing vision with action, passion with pragmatism, and creativity with discipline. This interplay ensures that businesses not only start strong but sustain growth.

Challenges are inevitable, but they are also opportunities in disguise. The ability to pivot, adapt, and innovate during setbacks separates successful entrepreneurs from the rest. Resilience, we've learned, is the cornerstone of success.

The Importance of Action, Resilience, and Passion

Dreams remain dormant without action. Taking the first step—whether it's building a prototype, launching a campaign, or setting up a lemonade stand—propels you forward. Action is not about perfection but progress, and every step builds momentum.

Entrepreneurship is a marathon, not a sprint. Setbacks are not signs of failure but opportunities to recalibrate and grow stronger. As this book has shown, setbacks often provide the spark for innovative ideas and meaningful change.

Passion fuels persistence. It keeps you going during long nights, unanswered emails, and moments of doubt. When aligned with purpose, passion transforms businesses into movements that inspire and attract others.

Your Lemonade Stand Can Become a Legacy

A lemonade stand may seem humble, but the principles it embodies—creativity, service, and value creation are the seeds of a legacy. Whether you're starting a small business or aspiring to scale globally, your actions can leave a lasting impact on your industry, community, and future generations.

Legacy is not defined by financial achievements alone, rather, it encompasses how one's work contributes to the upliftment and inspiration of others. By engaging in mentorship for emerging entrepreneurs, supporting local communities, and adopting sustainable practices, individuals can establish a legacy characterized by goodwill and positive influence.

Patagonia exemplifies its legacy through its commitment to environmental sustainability. Its profits serve a higher purpose, proving that businesses can thrive while doing good.

When your business reflects integrity, resilience, and purpose, it becomes a model for others. Share your journey, document your lessons, and mentor aspiring entrepreneurs. By doing so, you inspire the next wave of changemakers.

The grandest businesses often start with modest beginnings. Your lemonade stands—whether literal or metaphorical is a powerful starting point. What matters is your willingness to take the leap, however small.

Take Ownership

As we've explored throughout this book, success doesn't require perfection, but it does demand ownership of your dreams. Take responsibility for your ideas, act on them, and adapt as you go.

Stay Persistent

Obstacles will come, but with persistence and adaptability, you'll overcome them. Remember, every entrepreneur starts somewhere, and every legacy begins with a single step.

Final Exercise

Set one achievable goal you can act on today. Whether it's drafting a business plan, reaching out to a mentor, or testing your product, take the first step toward your entrepreneurial dream.

In this book, we've explored the entrepreneurial journey, from finding inspiration to leaving a legacy. Along the way, we've highlighted the importance of action, resilience, and passion—the essential ingredients for turning dreams into reality.

Your lemonade stand, no matter how small it starts, holds the potential to create a ripple effect. With every sale, innovation, and act of service, you can build something that inspires others and leaves an enduring impact.

As you close this book, remember: the world is waiting for your idea, your passion, and your vision. Take the lessons you've learned, start small, and think big. Your lemonade stand can become a legacy. Now, go and make your mark. You've got this!

References

Ring, J. (2018). *We Were Yahoo!: From Internet Pioneer to the Trillion-Dollar Loss of Google and Facebook.* Gatekeeper Press.

https://ryansrecycling.com/about/

https://www.linkedin.com/pulse/lemonade-stands-lesson-business-resilience-arturo-henriquez-dfhrc

https://hbr.org/1985/11/the-dark-side-of-entrepreneurship

https://stories.starbucks.com/leadership/howard-schultz/#:~:text=A%20year%20later%2C%20in%201983,Italian%20coffeehouse%20tradition%20to%20America.

https://thestoryexchange.org/sara-blakely-refused-fear-failure-stop/

https://www.linkedin.com/pulse/dreamers-journey-creating-disney-empire-dr-iman-razavi

https://www.v.org/people/kevin-plank/

https://www.meandthebees.com/pages/about-us#:~:text=Mikaila%20Ulmer%2C%20Founder%20and%20CEO,when%20she%20was%20only%20four.

https://www.jeremyutley.design/blog/try-brainspeedstormwriting

https://www.nytimes.com/2014/05/04/business/where-a-desk-just-gets-in-the-way.html

https://www.nexford.edu/insights/entrepreneurial-mindset

https://en.wikipedia.org/wiki/SpaceX_Mars_colonizatio n_program#:~:text=settlement%20of%20Mars.- ,SpaceX%20has%20stated%20its%20goal%20is%2 0to%20colonize%20Mars%20to,human%20species %20by%20becoming%20multiplanetary.

https://www.businessinsider.com/dropbox-founder- and-ceo-drew-houston-interview-2017-6

https://www.brainyquote.com/quotes/thomas_a_edison _132683

https://fs.blog/carol-dweck-mindset/

https://www.linkedin.com/posts/oliverkenyon_heres- how-warby-parker-transformed-a-frustration- activity-7148017741445189633-UNyI

https://en.wikipedia.org/wiki/History_of_Amazon#:~:tex t=Amazon%20was%20founded%20by%20Jeff,moni ker%20%22the%20everything%20store%22.

https://oxfordexecutive.co.uk/case-study-netflixs- transition-from-dvd-rental-to-streaming/

https://en.wikipedia.org/wiki/Slack_(software)

https://knowledge.insead.edu/strategy/growing- resilience-uncertain-times

https://www.dyson.com/james-dyson

https://thedecisionlab.com/reference- guide/philosophy/scamper#:~:text=SCAMPER%20 encourages%20people%20to%20take,to%20think% 20outside%20the%20box.

https://www.productmonk.io/p/instagram-pivot

https://asana.com/resources/pareto-principle-80-20-rule#:~:text=The%20Pareto%20principle%20states%20that,can%20make%20the%20most%20impact.

https://en.wikipedia.org/wiki/Lean_manufacturing

https://hollyc.medium.com/what-you-need-to-know-about-finding-and-keeping-a-mentor-3cb752303ec5

https://www.forbes.com/sites/chloesorvino/2017/05/18/swell-bottle-founder-sarah-kauss-americas-most-successful-self-made-women/

https://www.linkedin.com/pulse/coca-cola-story-unraveling-genius-behind-marketing-revolution-udara-luglc

https://envoy.com/ebooks/onsite-collaboration-drives-success

https://www.linkedin.com/posts/haythamm3wadallah_hard-work-beats-talent-when-talent-doesn-activity-7151191423579566085-1ytA

https://www.go-globe.com/mobile-web-traffic-statistics-infographic/#:~:text=Ten%20years%20ago%2C%20mobile%20traffic,2011%20to%20over%2054%25%20today.

https://www.forbes.com/councils/forbescoachescouncil/2021/04/07/anxiety-vs-relaxationrelabeling-anxiety-as-excitement/

https://www.business.com/articles/never-giving-up-9-entrepreneurs-and-millionaires-who-failed-at-least-once/

https://www.nielsen.com/insights/2018/what-sustainability-means-today/

https://www.prnewswire.com/news-releases/stella-artois-and-waterorg-with-the-support-of-co-founders-matt-damon-and-gary-white-launch-buy-a-lady-a-drink-to-help-stop-womens-journeys-to-collect-water-in-the-developing-world-300024179.html

https://www.youtube.com/watch?v=_-fdJzvpX60

www.ingramcontent.com/pod-product-compliance
Lightning Source LLC
Chambersburg PA
CBHW021847170526
45157CB00007B/2972